text
Harriet Lake

design concept
Larry Soule

photos
UPI: pp. 6, 26, 28, 30
GLOBE: pp. 14, 16, 22, 38, 44
Minneapolis Star & Tribune: p. 40

published by
Creative Education,
Mankato, Minnesota

ON STAGE FRANK SINATRA

Published by Creative Educational Society, Inc.,
123 South Broad Street, Mankato, Minnesota 56001
Copyright © 1976 by Creative Educational Society, Inc. International
copyrights reserved in all countries.
No part of this book may be reproduced in any form without written
permission from the publisher. Printed in the United States.
Distributed by
Childrens Press, 1224 West Van Buren Street, Chicago, Illinois 60607
Library of Congress Numbers: 75-39981   ISBN: 0-87191-482-4

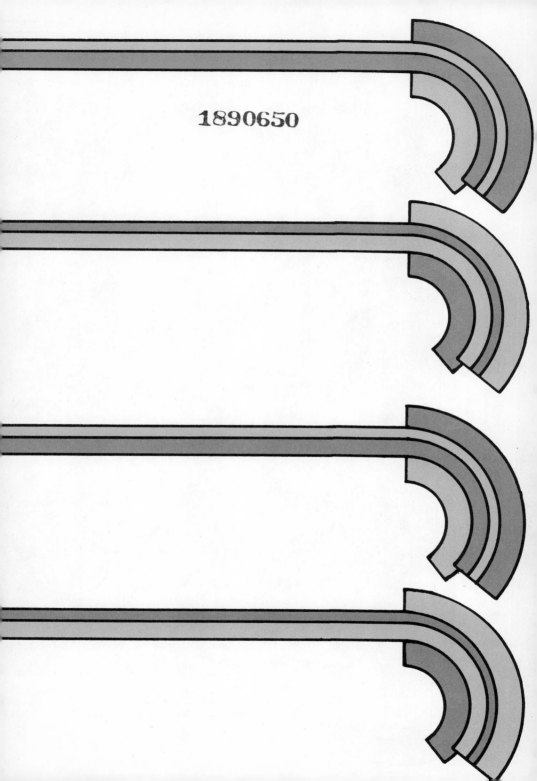

amateur

At 18, Frank Sinatra was a high school dropout. He was also unemployed, having quit his job as a truck loader. The Sinatras lived in a rough section of the dingy port city of Hoboken, New Jersey. In their neighborhood, gang fights were common. With a name like Francis Albert, a spindly frame, and a fondness for flashy clothes, Frank often had to defend himself against teenaged bullies who challenged him. Fist fights were tame; on occasion, Hoboken gangs fought with broken bottles and tire chains.

Music was rarely heard in Hoboken, except in church. Until Frank was a teenager, the family didn't own a radio. There were no musical instruments in the Sinatra home. Frank had never had a music lesson. Frank Sinatra didn't seem a likely candidate to succeed Bing Crosby as the country's most popular singer. But after hearing Crosby sing at a Jersey City vaudeville house, that became Frank's dream.

Frank's parents gave him no encouragement. His mother had been disappointed when he'd quit high school. She never gave up trying to convince him to go back to school, hoping this would lead to a steady job. When Dolly Sinatra found

7

a framed picture of Bing Crosby in her son's bedroom, she hurled a shoe at him.

Frank's father informed him that singing was for sissies. At one time or another, Martin Sinatra had been a boxer, a boilermaker and a bartender. Singing was not the kind of career he envisioned for his son.

But Frank was not discouraged by his parents' disapproval. Having made his decision to become a famous singer, he entered an amateur contest at a local theatre. To everyone's surprise but his own, he won. His prize was the chance to appear in a more important contest in a vaudeville theatre in New York. But when he got to New York, his confidence wavered.

Standing backstage at the New York Academy of Music before his number, he heard the noisy audience interrupt performers with shouts of, "Get the Hook!" Still in use on some amateur nights, the hook was a long pole with a curved end that came out of the wings and fitted around

the neck. It was used to yank unpopular performers off the stage.

Frank paced back and forth nervously, wondering if the hook would be used on him.. But once on stage, his nervousness disappeared. There were no catcalls from the audience. No hook appeared. But first prize went to someone else. Discouraged but still determined, Frank went home to New Jersey.

At first, he found work singing in local nightclubs. Then he was asked to sing with a band called the Hoboken Four. The group entered an amateur contest and won, giving them the chance to become part of a vaudeville touring unit. They traveled from city to city around the country, getting as far as California.

But the tour lasted only four months. There was a disagreement, and Frank left the group. Returning to New Jersey, he went back to singing on his own in local nightclubs. Although his salary was a meager $3.00 a night, he kept at it for three long years.

9

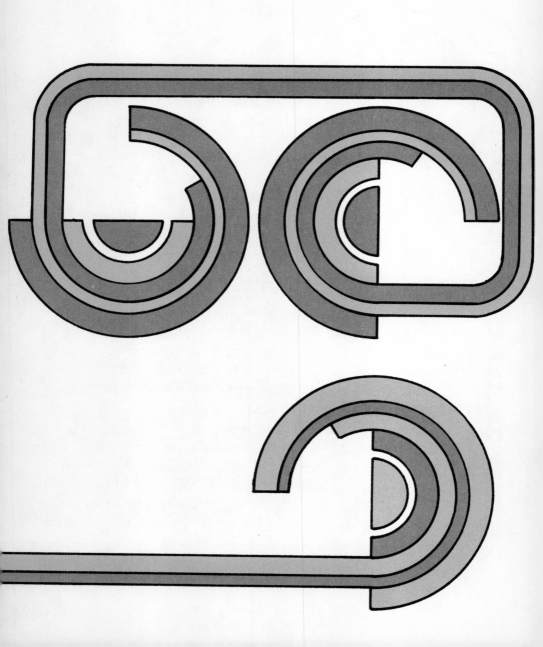

band singer

Frank Sinatra wanted to be more than a local nightclub singer. His goal was to become a vocalist with one of the big dance bands which dominated the music scene. Frank realized that the leaders of the famous bands weren't likely to notice him in the small club where he'd been working. He had to reach a wider audience.

Frank began hanging around several big New York radio stations. Whenever the stations' program directors emerged from their offices, Frank would be standing there. He persuaded them to let him sing on the air when no other programs were scheduled. He even offered to sing for free. Before long, he could be heard all over the dial, as many as 18 different times a week.

While singing free on the radio, Frank worked nights at a New Jersey nightclub called the Rustic Cabin. He sang solo and with a group, emceed, and even waited on tables — all for $15 a week. One evening Frank noticed Harry James in the audience. James, who had gained national recognition as a trumpeter with Benny Goodman's orchestra, had recently formed a band of his own. Frank wondered if he might be looking for a vocalist.

After the show, James left abruptly without speaking to anyone. But the next night, the bandleader was back. This time, he brought his manager with him and offered Sinatra a 2-year contract at $75 a week. Frank was jubilant. This seemed the chance he'd been waiting for.

But after a few months with Harry James, it seemed as though Frank's career was again bogged down. The James band was experiencing financial difficulties. The bandleader had to fire several musicians. But he kept Sinatra, even though reviews of his singing had been only lukewarm.

Just before Christmas, 1939, a friend of Tommy Dorsey's happened to hear Frank sing. Knowing Dorsey was looking for a new vocalist, he recommended Frank. "He's not much to look at," the friend warned Dorsey, "but he's got a sound." After listening to Sinatra, Tommy agreed. He made Frank an offer. Although Sinatra had worked only 6 months of his 2-year contract, Harry James generously agreed to let him go.

For Frank, the chance to leave the struggling James band for a berth with Tommy Dorsey was a dream come true. Of all the famous bands, Dorsey's was the one every vocalist wanted to sing with. While most other big bands featured mainly instrumental soloists, with Dorsey, the singer was the featured talent. Frank accepted Tommy's offer on the spot.

However, he left the James band with mixed emotions. Perhaps because of the difficulties the band had experienced, the musicians had become close friends. Frank did his last show with them one cold night in January, 1940. Then, as the musicians boarded the bus without him, he said goodby. "It was after midnight," he remembered later. "There was nobody around and I stood alone with my suitcase in the snow and watched the tail lights of the bus disappear. Then the tears started and I tried to run after the bus."

After he started singing with Tommy Dorsey's orchestra, Frank often had occasion to look back wistfully to his less hectic days with Harry James. He remembers the first few months with the new band as among the most miserable of his life. Audiences were not overly enthusiastic, and Frank found Tommy Dorsey, who was hot-tempered and sharp-tongued, to be a difficult man to work for. The Dorsey orchestra was one of the busiest. Between major engagements the band played at grueling one-night stands around the country. The long hours of traveling in cramped buses and the lack of sleep put all the musicians' tempers on edge.

Sinatra, who was short-tempered to begin with, soon got the reputation of a man always ready to fight. The provocation could be as slight as someone throwing popcorn on the stage or as direct as a drunk criticizing his singing. In either

14

case, Frank would fly off the bandstand in a rage, ready to do battle.

Frank's violent temper didn't hamper his growing popularity. In 1940, he edged out his old idol Bing Crosby in two separate polls to become rated as the country's most popular singer. However, the Dorsey band still ranked second to Glen Miller's. As an instrumental soloist, Dorsey found himself far down the list. Tommy was not pleased to find that his young vocalist had stolen the show. Friction between the two men increased. Finally, Frank left the band. He decided it was time to try to make it on his own.

soloist

Many popular band singers had tried to find fame as soloists. But since Bing Crosby, none had made it. The first few months Frank Sinatra was on his own, he began to wonder if he, too, had made a mistake. Few bookings were available, and a musicians' strike prevented him from making any records.

Finally Frank got a booking at the Mosque Theatre in Newark, New Jersey. His agent persuaded the director of the Paramount Theatre in New York to come and hear him sing. To the surprise of both men, the audience went crazy when Sinatra appeared. The theatre director was impressed, although he doubted New York audiences would be as enthusiastic. He did agree, though, to book Sinatra at the Paramount as an "Extra Added Attraction" on a bill headed by Benny Goodman's orchestra, then the top swing band in the country.

On opening night, December 30, 1942, Benny Goodman made no attempt to build up the "Extra Added Attraction." He introduced him by saying merely, "And now, Frank Sinatra." The audience responded with an unexpected roar of screams and applause. For a moment, Sinatra froze. Benny Goodman, also taken by surprise, turned around

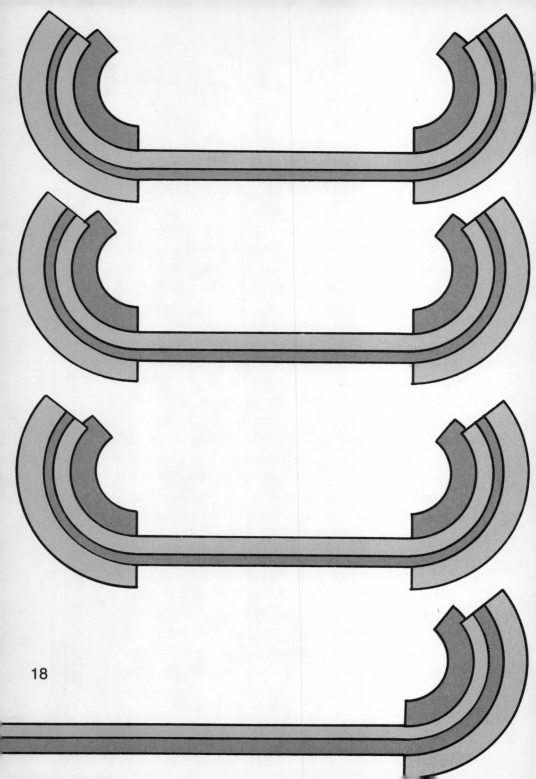

and stared at the audience. Frank recovered his composure first. He burst out laughing and started singing, "For Me and My Gal."

Sinatra stayed at the Paramount for eight roaring weeks. Each day the crowds of teenagers flocking to the theatre became larger and more hysterical. In their eagerness to get inside, fans trampled ushers and passersby. Those unable to get in milled around the theatre, hoping to get seats for the next performance. Usually they were disappointed. Once inside, fans stayed for show after show. One girl sat through 5 or 6 performances a day. By the end of Sinatra's engagement, she had attended 56 consecutive shows.

Other fans collected souvenirs. They picked up Sinatra's cigarette butts from hotel ashtrays and hair clippings from barbershop floors. One fan even broke into a house Frank had recently moved out of and made off with a bundle of old fan mail he'd thrown out.

The enthusiastic fans could sometimes be dangerous. One night Frank came out of a hotel about 1:00 a.m. after a late-night performance. A crowd of fans was waiting for him, eager for souvenirs. They began clutching at his clothing. In the melee, two girls grabbed opposite ends of his bow tie and began to pull. Neither of them could be persuaded to let go. In the resulting tug-of-war, their hero was nearly strangled to death.

After that incident, Sinatra hired a bodyguard to help smuggle him safely into hotels, restaurants, and theatres. Whenever he was in New York, he stayed at the Waldorf Astoria. In that hotel, there were 12 different ways of getting in and out. Sinatra once fooled fans by using the main exit. "It was unfair," one girl complained. "You never expect Frankie to use the front door."

Occasionally, Frank failed to outwit his admirers. Once he went to a small restaurant in Brooklyn for a spaghetti dinner, confident that no one would recognize him. Three thousand people gathered outside. Police had to break a small window in a washroom and hoist the disgruntled singer out of it into an alley, where they hustled him into a waiting taxi.

New York fans weren't the only ones who caused a commotion whenever Frank Sinatra appeared. In Boston, 3,000 girls mobbed his train. An equally large crowd met him in Chicago.

Eager fans broke several windows in the train, trying to get a glimpse of him.

Less than four months after he was billed as an "Extra Added Attraction," Frank Sinatra had become the hottest star in show business. His recording, "Sunday, Monday, and Always," sold a million copies. He sang on radio programs and in motion pictures. He made personal appearances at the best nightclubs, theatres and hotels. He even sang with symphony orchestras. Wherever he sang, box-office records were broken.

Soon all other singers were being compared to Sinatra. First there was a singer billed as the "Mexican Sinatra." Then the "Russian Sinatra" appeared, followed by "The Sinatra of Grand Opera," and "The Older Girl's Sinatra." One singer named Soo even called himself "Soonatra." Meanwhile, Sinatra himself was being billed as "The Voice that Thrills Millions." Later this was shortened to simply "The Voice."

Most popular singers were careful not to take sides on controversial issues. But Frank Sinatra stirred up controversy wherever he went. In 1944, he plunged into politics, campaigning enthusiastically for President Roosevelt. He gave pro-Roosevelt talks over the radio and spoke to huge audiences at county fairs across the country. Wherever Sinatra appeared, crowds gathered.

On one occasion, Thomas Dewey, Roosevelt's Republican opponent, was addressing a large crowd on Park Avenue in New York when Frank happened to pass by. In a matter of minutes, Dewey found himself without an audience. The crowd was trailing off down the street after Frank Sinatra.

Sinatra's effectiveness as a Democratic campaign worker did not endear him to those of his fans who happened to be Republicans. Friends warned him that his political activities were endangering his career. But Frank was adamant. "I believe that an entertainer's function is to entertain," he said, "but he is also a responsible citizen with the same rights and obligations as the next man. I feel it is the duty of every American citizen to help elect the candidates of his choice."

Sinatra stood equally firm in his battles against prejudice. Remembering the slights he had endured as a youngster because of his Italian heritage, Frank was always quick to protest prejudice of all kinds. Once he slugged the white owner of a lunch counter for refusing to serve a black musician. He stormed out of the christening of his son Franklin (named after President Roosevelt) because the priest refused to accept a Jewish godfather for the ceremony.

When he became a teenage idol, Frank saw a chance to influence young people's views on the racial issue. The only popular singer to speak out on such an explosive subject, Sinatra spoke in high school auditoriums all over the country. He pleaded with students not to dislike others because of their color or religion.

Eventually, Sinatra made a short film called "The House I Live In," urging religious and racial tolerance. He donated the proceeds to agencies involved in helping teenagers. In 1946 the film won a special Academy Award.

Not all Sinatra's battles were fought for noble causes. He argued with movie producers, cast members, and fans who happened to ask for his autograph. There were blowups with record company officials and recording technicians. But Sinatra reserved his hottest verbal blasts for members of the press who printed stories that offended him. He detested certain newspaper columnists. Occasionally he came to blows with some of them. One case ended up in court. To avoid a jail term, Sinatra had to pay the injured columnist a $9,000 settlement. Including lawyers' fees, that display of temper cost him a total of $25,000.

All these incidents, as well as the news that Frank had separated from his wife Nancy Barbato, and was pursuing sultry Hollywood star Ava Gardner, were reported in newspapers across the country. There were also rumors that Sinatra had been associating with gangster "Lucky" Luciano, a member of the Mafia. Although Sinatra vehemently denied the charge, the rumors were enough to raise further suspicions in the minds of many people who were becoming disgusted with Sinatra's image as a brawler.

sliding down

In the fall of 1948, Frank Sinatra was spotted in New York, walking slowly down Broadway, his collar up and his head bare. Four years earlier, he had tied up traffic whenever he appeared. Now no one even recognized him. Reviews of his movies had gone from bad to worse. Even more alarming, there was criticism of his singing.

For years, Frank had been locked into a frantic schedule of movie-making, recording sessions, radio programs, and personal appearances. His health and nerves had suffered, as well as his voice. By February, 1949, he was on the point of a breakdown. Even though he had a bad cold and was under a doctor's orders to stay in bed, Frank insisted on keeping a date at the Copacabana Club in New York.

At 2:30 a.m. the third show of the evening started. When Sinatra opened his mouth to sing, nothing came out. The audience grew silent. His face white, Frank whispered "good night" into the microphone and ran off-stage. Later, his voice failure was diagnosed as a throat hemorrhage.

For several months, Frank couldn't sing at all.

Ten years after he had burst onto the entertainment scene, it appeared Frank Sinatra's career as a singer was at an end. Attendance at his performances had dropped off sharply. At the Chez Paris club in Chicago, which could seat 1,200 people, the audience numbered only 150.

Sales of Sinatra's records dipped dangerously. Taste in popular music was shifting from romantic ballads to fast-paced country songs, folk music, and cool jazz. Frank Sinatra's records no longer appeared on the charts of top tunes. His recording contract was not renewed. His talent agency dropped him. CBS cancelled his television show. Film companies weren't making any offers.

Sinatra's personal life, too, was in a shambles. Having divorced his first wife, Nancy, Frank had married film star Ava Gardner. But their marriage also proved stormy. To top off his troubles Frank, who had always been a lavish spender, found himself in a financial pinch. The IRS notified him that there had been a mistake on his tax return and that he owed the government $109,996 in back taxes. The future looked bleak.

turning point

One day, Sinatra happened to pick up the best-selling novel, **From Here to Eternity.** As he read, he became increasingly excited. Frank knew the book would be made into a movie. He was convinced he was the one who should play the part of the tough little Italian-American soldier. "I knew Maggio," he said later. "I went to high school with him in Hoboken. I was beaten up with him. I might have been Maggio."

As soon as the screen rights to the book were purchased, Sinatra began badgering studio executives to let him play the part. "But it's an acting role, Frankie," they told him. "You're a singer."

"But it's me," he persisted. "Give me the part and you'll never be sorry."

Even when he heard the studio was testing big-name actors for the part, Frank kept begging for a screen test. He even offered to accept a much smaller salary than he'd gotten in years past. But the producers didn't seem interested. Weeks passed. Sinatra heard nothing.

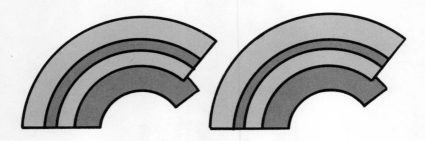

Finally an invitation for a screen test came. Frank was in Africa with Ava, who was doing a film there. Even though the studio didn't offer to pay for the 27,000-mile round trip to Hollywood and back, Frank did not hesitate. He caught the next plane.

Back in Hollywood, Frank went directly to the studio. The cameras were readied. The producer handed him a script. Frank handed it back. "I don't need this," he said. The producer shrugged, thinking Frank had no chance of getting the part anyway.

But as Frank began playing the scene, the producer suddenly became interested. Of all the actors he'd tested, Frank's portrayal of Maggio was by far the best. In fact, rarely had he seen such a brilliant performance from any actor. Gleefully, he whispered to the director, "If he's like that in the movie, it's a sure Academy Award." Sinatra got the part.

Sinatra won the predicted Oscar and increasing recognition as a serious actor, as well. Movie studios again began competing with each other to book Frank Sinatra for upcoming films. But now, instead of light singing parts, they were

offering him serious dramatic roles. In quick succession, Sinatra played a variety of comic characters and tragic heroes: a sadistic gunman trying to ·assassinate the President (in **Suddenly**), a canny gambler **(Guys and Dolls)**, a doctor **(Not as a Stranger)**, and a suave bachelor being maneuvered into marriage **(The Tender Trap)**.

But it was Sinatra's portrayal of the jazz drummer struggling to overcome his drug addiction in **The Man with the Golden Arm** that many felt was his finest acting achievement. Because of the subject, some critics found the movie itself "sordid" and "immoral," but all of them agreed that Sinatra's performance was outstanding.

While the movie was being produced, Frank threw himself totally into his work, arriving at the studio at 8:00 in the morning and working as many as 12 hours in front of the cameras. He lived his part, thinking of little else. He never needed to rehearse a scene. When it was time to shoot the difficult scene in which the addict tries to kick his habit and suffers the agonies of withdrawal, the director urged Frank to rehearse the scene a couple of times. He offered to do as many retakes as necessary. But Frank declined the

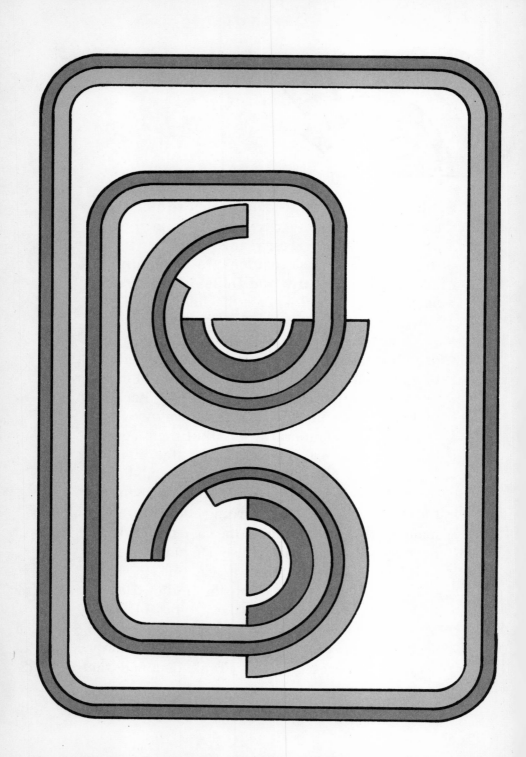

offer. He knew exactly how the drug addict would react. "Just keep those cameras grinding," he insisted. With no rehearsals, the scene was shot in one take.

Sinatra's triumph in films marked his comeback as a singer, as well. After his performance in **From Here to Eternity**, his records again began appearing on the "Hit Parade." In a 1954 poll of disc jockeys, Sinatra's "Young at Heart" was picked as the year's number 1 record, and his "Swing Easy" album was chosen as the number 1 LP. In 1955, he was named best male singer of the year.

Once again, Sinatra was back on top. His career seemed to be taking off in all directions. On television, he starred in a musical version of **Our Town.** ABC signed him for a $3 million, 13-segment T.V. series.

With fame and fortune again within his grasp, Sinatra glowed with confidence. "Man, I feel 8 feet tall," he told one reporter. "Everything is ahead of me. I'm on top of the world . . . The career is going ahead wonderfully. People are wonderful to me and I'm a happy, happy man."

Frank's exuberant mood was revealed in his music. Along with the romantic ballads he'd always sung, he began experimenting with jazzy, hard-driving numbers. Record promoters began creating a new image for him — the "Swinging Sinatra."

the clan

Sinatra's friends added to his image as a "swinger." His entourage, known as The Clan, included such well-known stars as Dean Martin, Sammy Davis, Jr., Peter Lawford, and Joey Bishop. Sinatra was called "The Leader." Clan gatherings were called "Summit Meetings."

The Clan often engaged in spirited high-jinks and practical jokes, heckling performers in night clubs and occasionally taking over the stage completely. Sometimes Clan members appeared together in movies. During the shooting of **Ocean's Eleven,** which was set in Las Vegas gambling casinos, the Clan gathered after hours and gave impromptu shows for the customers.

Clan members all deferred to Sinatra, their "Leader." They all dressed like him in dark suits and bow ties and tried to imitate him in every way possible, even to driving expensive sports cars exactly like his. The Clan insisted the whole thing was a joke, but some people questioned whether it was.

It was well-known that Clan members, who were powerful stars in their own right, would go along with any project their "Leader" favored.

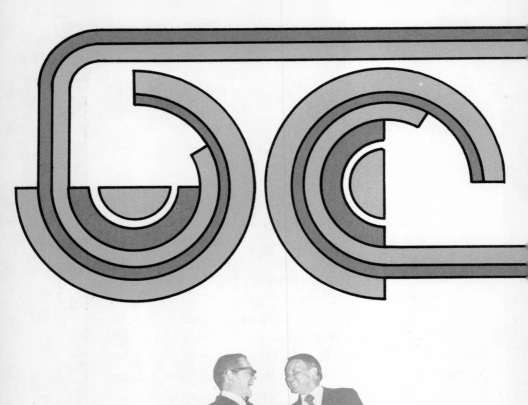

Sammy Davis, Jr. once jokingly described the Clan as "just a little group of ordinary guys that get together once a year to take over the entire world." Many people thought this wasn't far from the truth.

Frank Sinatra had become one of the most powerful men in Hollywood. His investment in numerous business enterprises totaled $25 million. By 1961, he owned a music publishing company and a record company (Reprise), as well as large shares of all the films he appeared in. There were rumors that he planned to form a talent agency, as well. Through these interests, he had a big part in deciding which actors were employed and which songs were published, recorded, and plugged. People began to speak of Hollywood as "a little place Frank Sinatra owns."

superstar

Over the years, Frank Sinatra became more and more involved with his business interests, though he still made occasional films and personal appearances. He told a reporter, "I see myself not so much an entertainer as a high-level executive, interested in business, perhaps in directing and producing films . . . and that's the way I want it to be."

Yet Sinatra still exerted a powerful pull at the box office, and he still performed to capacity crowds whenever he made personal appearances. The fans were slightly older than in years past but just as enthusiastic. When Frank appeared in Atlantic City in 1959, a customer offered him $50 for one of his cigarette butts. A forty-year-old woman threw herself in front of his limousine, pleading hysterically, "Run me over, Frankie!" Although the popular music scene was increasingly dominated by rock 'n roll, Frank Sinatra remained the "Love Voice of America," a reminder to those approaching middle age of the "good music" of their youth.

In 1960, Sinatra's prestige as the nation's most durable super-star was further enhanced. President Kennedy asked him to stage a show for his

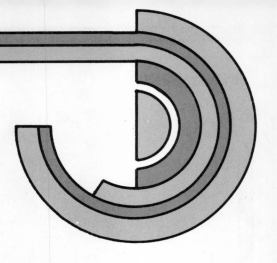

inaugural celebration. Sinatra had met Kennedy
through Peter Lawford, a Clan member who also
happened to be the President's brother-in-law.
Frank greatly admired Kennedy and had cam-
paigned enthusiastically for him, speaking at
fund-raisers and benefits. The invitation to pro-
duce the inaugural show was one of the greatest
thrills of his life.

As it turned out, the gala event was marred by
bad weather. It snowed on the day of the celebration. Streets of the capital were blocked by
stalled cars. The President and Mrs. Kennedy
finally succeeded in reaching the concert hall.
But they found that the hundred-piece orchestra,
the conductor and the soloists were missing, as
well as most of the audience.

Leonard Bernstein was finally rescued from
his stalled car by a White House limousine and
rushed to the hall to conduct the opening fanfare.
Mahalia Jackson, Nat "King" Cole, Ella Fitz-
gerald, and other soloists eventually arrived.

Even though many were lacking special costumes, they gave inspired performances. At the end of the concert, the President-elect rose and offered a tribute. "We're all indebted to a great friend, Frank Sinatra," he said. "Tonight we saw excellence." For Frank, it was a moment of triumph. The streets of Hoboken seemed far away.

Later, controversy over Sinatra's rumored Mafia associations, questionable business dealings, and Clan high-jinks, led to a cooling of the President's friendship with Sinatra. But Frank still cherishes Kennedy's memory. In his Palm Springs home, there is a plaque on one of the bedroom doors that reads,

JOHN F. KENNEDY
Slept Here
November 6th and 7th, 1960

Sinatra also points out to visitors the red phone in his study which Kennedy used for calls to Washington.

september of his years

In 1965, Frank Sinatra celebrated his 50th birthday. He was in a mood for reminiscing. The songs he recorded that year, "How Old Am I," "It Was A Very Good Year," "It Gets Lonely Early," indicate that he was aware of approaching a turning point in his life.

But Frank was not yet ready to retire to a rocking chair — or even to the golf course. He embarked on an ambitious series of personal appearances. With the Count Basie band, he made a cross-country concert tour. It was the first time in 20 years that he'd gone out on tour with a band. Every concert was sold out. At the Newport Jazz Festival, Frank received the most applause of any performer.

Having proved he was still able to draw capacity crowds, Sinatra proceeded to accumulate successes in other areas. His movie **Von Ryan's Express** was both a critical success and a hit at the box office. His records, "Strangers in the Night," "That's Life," and "Something Stupid," all climbed to number one on the record charts. 1965 was, indeed, a "Very Good Year."

45

Ten years afterwards, as Sinatra approaches his 60th birthday, another such burst of recording and performing seems unlikely. Sinatra says he has retired. However, he still flies to his Los Angeles office daily to oversee his vast business empire. Still restless and impatient, he is always on the move. A friend once said of Sinatra, "So long as he's frantic, he's relaxed . . . when he begins to relax, he gets frantic."

Even though he knows his voice isn't in top form anymore, Sinatra sometimes can't resist the lure of the recording studio. He constantly experiments with new arrangements and accompaniments. Sometimes he abandons the romantic ballads he's always preferred to try out new kinds of music, such as rock and bossa nova.

Since the break-up of his brief marriage to actress Mia Farrow, Sinatra has lived alone in his luxurious house in Palm Springs. These days, he is calmer and in better control of his temper, more apt to shrug off criticism than start a fight. But he can still deliver stinging verbal blasts on occasion. And he retains his powerful personal magnetism. When Sinatra enters a room, all eyes turn toward him.

Frank Sinatra may not have achieved the inner peace that has always eluded him. But he has the satisfaction of knowing that he's always been true to himself. Right or wrong, he has said and done what he believed in. "My Way" has been a lonely way, but an honest one.